ASIA

Troll Associates

ASIA

by Louis Sabin
Illustrated by Allan Eitzen

Troll Associates

Library of Congress Cataloging in Publication Data

Sabin, Louis.
   Asia.

   Summary: A brief overview of the geography of the
largest continent in the world.
   1. Asia—Description and travel—1951-   —Juvenile
literature. [1. Asia—Geography] I. Eitzen, Allan, ill.
II. Title.
DS10.S24   1985   950   84-10559
ISBN 0-8167-0274-8 (lib. bdg.)
ISBN 0-8167-0275-6 (pbk.)

Asia has more land, more people, and more wealth than any other continent on Earth. The Asian continent covers about one third of the world's land surface. It stretches from the barren Arctic wastelands of Siberia in the north all the way to the tropical Indonesian islands on the equator.

In the west, Asia is separated from Europe by the Ural Mountains. In the southwest, it is touched by the Mediterranean Sea and the Red Sea. To the south is the Indian Ocean. And to the east is the vast Pacific Ocean.

8

This huge land mass called Asia is filled with extremes. Mount Everest, in the section of China called Tibet, is the highest mountain in the world. Its snowcapped peak is more than five miles above sea level. The air at the top is so thin that climbers cannot survive there without breathing from oxygen tanks. Asia also boasts the lowest point in the world—nearly a quarter of a mile below sea level. It is the Dead Sea, on the border of Israel and Jordan.

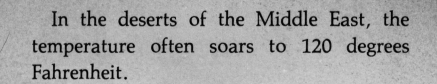

In the deserts of the Middle East, the temperature often soars to 120 degrees Fahrenheit.

In northern Siberia, it may plunge to nearly 100 degrees below zero.

*Arabian
Desert*

But perhaps Asia's greatest extreme is its population. Even if all of the continent were suitable for people to live on, it would still be crowded. However, much of the land isn't fit for people to live on. Few people are able to survive in the parched Arabian and Gobi Deserts, in the snow-blanketed mountains of Tibet and Nepal, or on the bleak Siberian tundra.

Siberian Tundra

Gobi
Desert

Mountains of Tibet

Mountains of Nepal

This means that the population of Asia—
over two-and-a-half-billion people, or more
than half of all the people in the world—
must live on just a small part of the
continent, near the coasts and in mountain
and river valleys.

North

Central

East

Southwest

South

Southeast

The climate, land features, people, and way of life vary widely from one part of Asia to another. The continent can be divided into six large regions: Southwest, South, Southeast, East, North, and Central or Middle Asia.

14

The Southwest region of Asia is made up of the countries that are located on and near the Arabian Peninsula. More than two thirds of the people who live here are farmers. They live in small villages near the seacoasts, in mountain valleys, and along the Tigris and Euphrates Rivers, where there is enough water to produce crops.

15

But much of the land of Southwest Asia is desert. For thousands of years, the only people to live in the dry deserts were nomads, or wanderers, who raised small flocks of sheep and herds of goats and camels. The majority of the population in this region was poor, had no medical care, was uneducated, and faced the future with little hope of improving their lives.

Then came oil, gushing up from the sand. Billions of barrels of oil poured out of the wells, and billions of dollars poured into the oil-producing nations. This sudden wealth has been used for hospitals and schools, roads and power plants. It has been used to build modern cities and to feed the people. It has also brought foreign technology and luxuries and ideas that are upsetting age-old ways and traditions.

In most of the oil-rich countries of Southwest Asia, the governments are trying to deal with the problems brought on by the sudden wealth and sudden changes. They are moving cautiously so that traditional ways of life will not be swept away all at once.

The second major region is South Asia. It covers about a tenth of the continent, but it is home to about a third of the Asian population. The largest and most populated country in this region is India. Here, the people are mainly poor farmers, growing rice, cotton, tea, nuts, grains, rubber, sugar cane, and spices. But most of the farms are tiny, and the land is not very fertile.

In addition, the farming methods are primitive. All the work is done by hand or with the help of animals, just as it has been done for hundreds and hundreds of years. As a result, not enough food is produced to feed the enormous population.

The third major region, Southeast Asia, is made up of a peninsula and a series of islands that stretch out toward Australia. Here there are thick forests, fertile soil, and abundant rainfall. Most of the people make their living by farming. But most farms are small, and the work is done by hand. Rice is the major crop, but other crops are grown, including coffee, tea, sugar cane, tobacco, fruits and vegetables, and rubber.

East Asia is made up mainly of eastern China, Japan, Taiwan, and North and South Korea. China has an agricultural economy, like most other countries in this region. Although it is one of the world's largest countries in total area, China still faces the challenge of feeding its people.

Only a small portion of the land in China can be farmed easily. The rest of the land is mountainous, desert, or dry and rocky land. Until recently, farming methods were backward, and Chinese industry was limited. This meant that China did not produce enough food for itself and had no manufactured goods to trade for foreign food.

Then came a series of changes that are rapidly modernizing China. Free education became available for the first time in Chinese history, as did medical care for the many millions who live in the countryside. At the same time, modern methods and machinery were applied to farming. Now China is no longer a starving nation.

However, the Chinese people still do not enjoy a high standard of living by Western standards. The country's resources are

primarily being used for major projects, including the building of factories, power stations, and machinery of all kinds; the mining of China's vast store of minerals, such as coal, iron, tin, and tungsten; and the gradual improvement of agricultural methods.

Japan is the most industrialized of all Asian countries. Over one hundred million people live in Japan—that's five times the population of the state of California. But this island country is smaller than California, and much of its land is rocky, mountainous, and difficult to farm.

Nonetheless, the Japanese enjoy their high standard of living for several reasons. They use every inch of farm land. They maintain a large and efficient fishing industry. In addition, they export high-quality manufactured goods, and use part of the profits to buy whatever food they cannot grow in their own country.

For hundreds of years, Japan has exported silk, pearls, and tea. These are still important sources of income for this island nation. But high-technology products, such as cameras, television and radio sets, stereo equipment, digital watches, cars, and computers, have made Japan one of the leading trade nations in the world.

The other countries in the eastern region of Asia are North and South Korea and Taiwan—an island nation off the coast of mainland China. Taiwan has an agricultural economy. Agriculture and industry are equally important in South Korea. And North Korea's economy is based on industry.

The fifth region of Asia is the Central or Middle section of the continent. It includes the rest of China plus the country of Mongolia. The land here is high in elevation and is suited more to raising livestock than to farming or industry. It is a region of rugged mountains (including Mount Everest in the Himalayas), of rocky plateaus, and of barren deserts, such as the huge Gobi in southern Mongolia.

The sixth and final region of the continent is North Asia. It stretches across the continent from the Bering Sea and Pacific Ocean to the Ural Mountains in the west—where Asia meets Europe. It is made up entirely of Russian territory. The most populated part of Russia, however, lies on the other side of the Urals—in Europe.

North Asia accounts for about forty percent of the Asian continent. But in spite of its huge size, it has less than three percent of the population of Asia. A few of the people hunt, trap, or herd such animals as cattle, sheep, or reindeer. The rest of the population works on farms in the countryside or in factories inside the cities.

Asia might be referred to as the "continent of religions." From western Asia came Islam, Christianity, and Judaism. From southeastern Asia came Buddhism and Hinduism. And from eastern Asia came Shintoism, Taoism, and Confucianism. All the great religions of the world began in Asia and continue to be practiced there.

Asia is a continent where old and new exist side by side—where languages, religions, governments, and traditions are as different and varied as the land itself. Asia accounts for a third of all the land on Earth, stretching from the barren Arctic in the north to the tropical islands in the south, from the shores of the Mediterranean Sea in the west to the shores of the Pacific Ocean in the east. It is a huge and fascinating land—the largest continent in the world—Asia.